New Ways for Work Workbook

Personal Skills for Productive Relationships

By

Bill Eddy, LCSW, Esq. and L. Georgi DiStefano, LCSW

HIGH CONFLICT INSTITUTE PRESS
Scottsdale, Arizona

Publisher's Note: This publication is designed to provide accurate and authoritative information about the subject matters covered. It is sold with the understanding that neither the authors nor publisher are rendering legal, mental health, medical or other professional services, either directly or indirectly. If expert assistance, legal services or counseling is needed, the services of a competent professional should be sought. Neither the authors nor the publisher shall be liable or responsible for any loss or damage allegedly arising as a consequence of your use or application of any information or suggestions in this book.

Copyright © 2015 by Bill Eddy and L. Georgi DiStefano
High Conflict Institute Press
7701 E. Indian School Rd., Ste. F
Scottsdale, AZ 85251
www.hcipress.com

Cover design by Gordan Blazevik
Book Interior design by Kristen Onesti

All rights reserved.

No part of this book may be reproduced, scanned, or distributed in any printed or electronic form without the express written permission of the publisher. Failure to comply with these terms may expose you to legal action and damages for copyright infringement. A client or individual who has purchased this workbook may make copies of blank exercises for his or her own personal use. They may not be sold or provided to others.

ORDERING MORE COPIES
Bulk rates are available on orders of 10 or more copies. Please contact HCI Press at 1-888-986-4665 or www.hcipress.com for pricing and to place orders.

Printed in the United States of America

Negotiation and mediation expert William A. ("Bill") Eddy is president of the High Conflict Institute and a certified family law specialist. Prior to becoming a lawyer, Eddy worked as a licensed clinical social worker. He speaks throughout the U.S. and internationally about high-conflict personalities and provides consultation and training on workplace issues. He is also the author of several books on managing and responding to high-conflict people. He lives in San Diego, California.

L.Georgi DiStefano is a licensed clinical social worker with extensive experience as a therapist, Employee Assistance provider, management consultant, and a popular speaker on workplace conflict resolution. She has authored several books and articles, and has directed mental health and substance abuse programs. She lives in San Diego, California.

Bill and Georgi are coauthors of *It's All Your Fault at Work! Managing Narcissists and Other High-Conflict People* (Unhooked Books Publishing, 2015).

Learn more about the authors at www.highconflictinstitute.com.

CONTENTS

Jobs today are about relationships: Relationships with clients, customers, co-workers, managers, the company, and competitors. Yet the personal skills needed to manage these relationships are changing rapidly. It's common knowledge that stress from dealing with other people in the workplace is one of the largest factors affecting job dissatisfaction.

New Ways for Work: The Workbook was developed to give employees and managers training for modern work relationships while in a relationship – a coaching relationship – with an emphasis on practicing four key self-management skills: *managed emotions, flexible thinking, moderate behavior,* and *checking yourself.* Using numerous writing and discussion exercises, this workbook assists an employee or manager who wants to improve his or her workplace relationship skills while working with a coach in up to 12 coaching sessions.

IMPROVING YOUR WORKPLACE SKILLS

Some people will be learning or strengthening these four skills because they have had difficulty in a workplace relationship and were referred for this coaching to improve their skills. They may have been in "high-conflict" situations where they and/or others used the following negative behaviors:

All-or-nothing thinking (seeing oneself as perfect, others as all-bad)

Unmanaged emotions (frequent yelling, blaming, crying, dramatics)

Extreme behaviors (threats of violence, yelling, stealing, false reports, spreading rumors, etc.)

Blaming others (focusing on others' behavior; not taking responsibility for own actions)

In many high-conflict situations, only one person has these characteristics and other people are trying hard to be reasonable. In other high-conflict situations, two or more people have some of these characteristics, although one may be more extreme than the other. In order to avoid being seen as a "high-conflict person," learning and strengthening the skills in this workbook will help you do the opposite of the above behaviors.

ADVANCING IN YOUR CAREER

Others learning the skills in this workbook are doing so because they want to advance in their career. Employees and managers who wish to "move up" will benefit themselves by learning and strengthening the use of the same four self-management skills. This is because these skills help you concentrate on your goals even when facing resistance from others or other distractions. These skills will also help you assist other employees in managing difficult situations, without becoming overwhelmed yourself.

Whether you are seeking to improve your skills or advance in your career, we believe you will enjoy learning these skills and find them useful anywhere with anybody – even neighbors, friends, family, and strangers.

The 4 "New Ways" Skills are:

Flexible thinking · Managed emotions · Moderate behaviors · Checking yourself

By practicing these skills, you will be more able to stay calm in a conflict, find solutions to problems, and influence others in a positive direction.

YOUR COACH

Your coach may be an Employee Assistance Professional, a mental health professional or someone else. Throughout this workbook, we refer to your "coach," which could mean any of these roles. The main idea is that they are coaching you to strengthen your own skills rather than to solve problems for you. The type of coaching involved with this workbook is often known as "skill building." With this method, your coach will focus more on the future and less on the past, and more on what to do and less on how you feel about it. Feel free to ask questions and discuss your expectations with your coach, so that this method can be most effective for you.

A COGNITIVE-BEHAVIORAL METHOD

The method of learning contained in this book includes changing some of your thinking as well as some of your behavior. This type of approach is called a "Cognitive-Behavioral" method. This involves simple practice exercises in writing to help change some of your thinking to a more positive frame of mind. It also involves discussions with your coach to help change some of your behavior – how you interact with others -- by practicing with your coach. Cognitive-Behavioral methods are very well respected and researched types of approach. They are known to be effective, even when you do a lot of the work on your own.

WHY A WORKBOOK?

Cognitive-Behavioral methods often use writing exercises to help us remember and strengthen our use of knowledge and new skills, as well as helping us practice them in person. It appears to help us build stronger pathways in our brains for solving problems more automatically in the future, just like practicing a sport or a musical instrument. This workbook belongs to you and is intended to be confidential, so you can refer back to it in the future to reinforce the skills you will learn.

The workbook also helps focus the coaching sessions, while leaving time for you to raise other issues during part of each session.

You may find it is easier to communicate and solve problems with others who have learned the same skills contained in this workbook, such as using the same methods for email responses and proposing solutions to problems.

Some of the writing exercises can be done before a coaching session, while most of them will be done during or after a coaching session. It helps to read ahead about the topic for the next session. Consult with your coach about any homework between sessions. The workbook is designed to help focus and remember your coaching discussions. It's up to you!

NOW, LET'S GET STARTED!

New Ways for Work
Individual Coaching

SESSION 1: PROBLEMS OR ISSUES TO DISCUSS

During this session, you and your Employee Assistance Professional (EAP), counselor, or coach will get acquainted. He or she will ask you questions about the problems or issues you want to address in the coaching and also discuss your general goals for the coaching. You will also discuss whether how many sessions of *New Ways for Work* coaching you would like, up to 12 sessions.

Your coach will also ask some questions about your background, in order to more fully understand the problem or issue you want help with and where it fits into your life – including some of the challenges you have faced in the past that may help in coaching for the future. If you wish, you can prepare a written page or two about your background, or just wait to meet with your coach and talk about it.

PROBLEMS OR ISSUES TO DISCUSS

Write one to two problems or issues here that you would like to discuss with your Coach:

Pick one problem or issue and explain it in more detail. Let's call this your "Identified Problem" or "Issue":

Describe or discuss in general terms your initial thoughts about what your goal(s) are for the coaching in relation to the Identified Problem or Issue you have selected:

_____

_____

_____

_____

Describe or discuss what it would look like in your daily life, if you accomplished the goal(s) described above in relation to your Identified Problem or Issue:

_____

_____

_____

_____

_____

_____

Think of anything else you would like to remember to tell your Coach in regard to your Identified Problem or Issue:

_____

_____

_____

_____

_____

SESSION SUMMARY

Write a key thought(s) that came out of this session that you would like to remember:

_____

_____

_____

_____

_____

THE NEW WAYS SKILLS ARE:

Flexible Thinking

Managed Emotions

Moderate Behaviors

Checking Yourself

FLEXIBLE THINKING

We are constantly facing new situations that may never have occurred in our lives before, or even in the world before. One of the biggest barriers to success in a changing world is all-or-nothing thinking. What we need is flexible thinking for new ways of solving problems in new situations. All-or-nothing thinking keeps us stuck in old ways and over-reacting to change, while flexible thinking helps us keep thinking of new ideas and trying them out until something works.

HERE ARE SOME COMMON EXAMPLES OF ALL-OR-NOTHING THINKING:

"My life isn't working. I have to change everything that I do."

"I'm doing an excellent job. There's nothing I could improve."

"Everyone is against me. There's nothing I can do."

"Everyone should see things my way."

"I'm perfect as I am. There is nothing I can learn from this coach."

"Everything I do is wrong. This coach will save me."

"Things were wonderful. Now they're horrible!"

Write a *realistic* statement that is not "all-or-nothing thinking" that relates to your life:
For example: "I can learn new ways of doing things, regardless of how I did things in the past."
Or: "A co-worker may be able to change some of their workplace behavior, if I change mine. Let's see."

_____

_____

_____

_____

Write a *realistic* statement that is not "all-or-nothing thinking" that relates to your Identified Problem or Issue:

_____

_____

Discuss with your coach why you think that flexible thinking is helpful or unhelpful, or in what types of situations it could be helpful or unhelpful. Write an example of when flexible thinking could be helpful in addressing your Identified Problem or Issue:

_____

_____

_____

_____

Discuss with your coach a statement you can practice to remind yourself to use flexible thinking in the future, and a situation where you can practice flexible thinking this week. Write the statement here. Keep it short and easy to remember.

_____

_____

_____

THINKING INFLUENCES EMOTION INFLUENCES BEHAVIOR

Flexible thinking is at the center of managing emotions and keeping our behavior moderate. Many cognitive scientists believe that our thoughts lead to our emotions, which then leads to our behavior. With this in mind, you may be able to change how you feel and how you act by simply changing how you *think* about something.

For example, Paul is facing a tight deadline on a project this week. He feels stressed and starts thinking it's hopeless to meet this deadline, then he starts feeling angry about his workload in general and he shoves the papers on his desk onto the floor. Paul's *all-or-nothing* thinking led him to feel angry, which led him to feel so frustrated that he shoved his papers – which will take a while to re-organize – and make it harder to get done on time.

Instead, suppose that Paul had responded to his thinking that "it's hopeless," by telling himself to use his *flexible thinking* – that there's more than one solution to most problems and thinking about what alternatives he might have. He could say one or more of the following to himself:

Who can I talk to about changing the deadline?

Is there someone who could help me finish the project on time?

Can I change my priorities to make more room for this project this week?

I want to meet this deadline, but it's not the end of the world and it's not worth throwing things around and stressing myself out.

Just thinking about these alternatives will calm him down. He feels better because of these thoughts, which help him feel less hopeless. Not perfect, of course, but less hopeless. Now, he can look at how to solve his problem rather than just over-reacting and feeling worse and behaving badly. Here's how this looks in terms of influencing his own feelings and behavior by how he tells himself to think:

ALL-OR-NOTHING THINKING:

"It's hopeless" → "Now I'm really angry" → Shoving papers off the desk

Compared to:

FLEXIBLE THINKING:

"There's more than one solution to this problem"

↓

"I don't feel as stressed"

↓

"I'm going to talk to someone about this deadline"

As you can see, simply changing what you think (what you tell yourself – often known as your "self-talk") can make a huge difference in how you feel and how you behave.

SOMEONE YOU KNOW

Think of someone in your life who often uses all-or-nothing thinking. Write an example of what he/she would say or think:

_____

_____

_____

Write a new flexible thinking way that he/she could speak or think in the future on this subject:

_____

_____

_____

Remember, this is just a practice exercise to help you learn new ways of flexible thinking. So don't really tell the other person to think differently. That's their job. Focus on yourself now.

YOURSELF

Think of an example of all-or-nothing thinking you have sometimes. Write them here:

1. _____

_____

_____

2. _____

_____

_____

Write a flexible way that you could speak or think differently from what you wrote above:

1. _____

_____

_____

2. _____

_____

_____

MANAGED EMOTIONS

Upset emotions are normal in threatening situations no matter where you are, who you are, or who you are with. Yet being unable to manage our upset emotions can distract us from achieving our goals and create new problems for us, such as with those around us. Unmanaged emotions can make our lives a lot worse – even in just a split second. So learning to manage our emotions – even when times are tense – can make a big difference in our success at work. Learning how to stay calm in a crisis or how to calm yourself down after a stressful moment can make a huge difference in today's work world.

Here are some examples of unmanaged emotions that get people into trouble:

Yelling at co-workers.

Making threats to hurt someone on the job.

Bursting into tears around co-workers.

Refusing to cooperate with a manager out of anger.

Yelling at a difficult customer out of frustration.

Giving the silent treatment to a supervisor or co-worker.

Think of an example when you managed your emotions in a stressful situation. Write them down here:

_____

_____

_____

_____

_____

_____

_____

_____

Now, think of a situation in regard to your Identified Problem or Issue when you were under stress and you didn't manage your emotions very well. Write it here:

ONE WAY TO MANAGE OUR EMOTIONS

Tell yourself an encouraging statement

In the Olympics, most of the athletes learn to tell themselves encouraging statements while they are in the middle of extremely difficult challenges and millions of people are watching, especially when things are going badly and they are feeling very stressed or upset. These statements help them keep their cool.

Think of an encouraging statement you can tell yourself to get through an upsetting time related to your Identified Problem or Issues:

For example: "You can do it!"

Or: "I got through a worse situation last year! I'll get through this too!"

Write down one or more that you like:

Think of a stressful situation in the coming week in regard to your Identified Problem or Issue when telling yourself this encouraging statement might help you stay calm. **Discuss it with your coach.**

MODERATE BEHAVIORS

In the modern work world, moderate behaviors help us the most. Extreme behaviors can make things worse. You could have to spend a lot of time trying to fix the damage of extreme behaviors. Even extreme behavior in response to someone else's extreme behavior can make things worse. Here are some examples of extreme behaviors:

Insulting a customer

Insulting a manager

Insulting a co-worker

Storming out of a room in anger

Pushing a co-worker

Throwing something at a co-worker

Threatening to hit a co-worker

Stealing from the company

Writing a nasty email to anyone at work

Give an example of how an extreme behavior got someone into trouble:

_____

_____

_____

Think of an example of how you used a moderate behavior when you *felt* like using an extreme behavior. Write it here:

_____

_____

_____

_____

Think of a situation related to your Identified Problem or Issue that's coming up soon in which you may be tempted to use an extreme behavior. Think of a moderate behavior you could use instead and write it here:

_____

_____

_____

_____

_____

_____

CHECKING YOURSELF

From time to time, ask yourself if you are using these skills:

Flexible Thinking

Managed Emotions

Moderate Behavior

It's easy to forget to use these skills in the middle of discussing problems or difficult situations. If you are facing a change, it can help to remind yourself to use these skills going into a situation – to "Check Yourself."

HOMEWORK

Select another problem from your Identified Problem or Issue list, or come up with a new one. We will use this problem to help you practice the skills we have been discussing.

The prcblem is:

All-or-nothing thoughts concerning this problem would be:

Flexible thoughts concerning this problem are:

In relation to this problem, an example of unmanaged emotions would be:

In relation to this problem, an example of managed emotions would be:

_____

_____

_____

An example of extreme behavior in relation to this problem could be:

_____

_____

_____

_____

An example of moderate behavior in relation to this problem on my part would be:

_____

_____

_____

An encouraging statement that would help me in handling this problem successfully is:

_____

_____

_____

A realistic expectation for problem resolution in regard to this issue is:

1.   50% IMPROVEMENT

2.   20% IMPROVEMENT

3.   10% IMPROVEMENT

Explain why you selected the percentage you did.

_____

_____

_____

_____

REMEMBER TO BRING THIS HOMEWORK TO YOUR NEXT SESSION!

Whether this is your last session or you are continuing with more sessions, this will be a review of what you have learned so far and an opportunity to plan for the future. This session ends with setting personal goals to help you apply these skills to your own situation in the future.

The following are four General Goals for you to think about, so that you can write down some Personal Goals for yourself to go under each one:

To use flexible thinking in dealing with difficult situations.

To manage my upset emotions during difficult situations.

To use moderate behaviors with other employees and managers.

To validate my own strengths and personal qualities.

HERE'S A LIST OF SOME IDEAS FOR PERSONAL GOALS:

"To practice flexible thinking when a co-worker is blaming me."

"To manage my emotions when a manager is publically criticizing my actions."

"To respond with moderate behaviors when my customers send angry emails."

"To get my team to listen to me when I make workplace suggestions."

"To protect my team from other people's comments and behavior."

Think of Personal Goals for Yourself, under each of the General Goals below. Discuss your ideas with your coach, then write a Personal Goal under each General Goal.

Then, write something you have already learned under each goal.

To use flexible thinking in dealing with difficult situations.

My personal goal: _____

_____

_____

_____

What I have learned so far: _____

_____

_____

_____

_____

To manage my upset emotions during difficult situations.

My personal goal: _____

_____

_____

_____

_____

What I have learned so far: _____

_____

_____

_____

To use moderate behaviors with other employees, managers and clients/customers.

My personal goal: _____

_____

_____

_____

_____

What I have learned so far: _____

_____

_____

_____

To validate my own strengths and personal qualities.

My personal goal: _____

_____

_____

_____

What I have learned so far: _____

_____

_____

_____

REALISTIC EXPECTATIONS

Discuss with your coach a reasonable expectation for utilizing these four skills with your Identified Problem or Issue in the future.

How much do you think your situation will improve? _____ 50% _____ 20% _____ 10%

Discuss with your coach why 100% improvement is not realistic.

If you are finishing your coaching sessions with this third session, discuss how you can remember your goals for the future – especially in terms of your Identified Problem or Issue.

THE FUTURE

Discuss with your coach how you picture yourself using these skills in the future. Discuss how you will "Check Yourself" from time to time to remember to use these skills when you are under stress.

Write something you learned from this discussion:

_____

_____

_____

If you are going to have more sessions, throughout *New Ways for Work* you and your coach can look back on these personal goals to see if you are learning what you want to learn. You can change or add to these goals if something more meaningful comes up in the coaching. The goals are meant to guide you, not rule your life. But remember, these are your goals, so make sure to bring them up in your discussions of the skills described in this manual in each session.

Congratulations! You have finished three sessions of *New Ways for Work* coaching!

To strengthen your flexible thinking, apply what you have learned so far to the following scenarios and discuss them with your coach:

Joe (who has an excellent attendance record) was ten minutes late to work one morning when one of his most important customers called. Mary, the receptionist, took the call and told the customer she had no idea where Joe was and transferred the call to a rival sales associate. Was this all-or- nothing thinking? If so, what could Mary have done that would show flexible thinking?

Write your responses here:

_____

_____

_____

_____

Alice and Robert worked very hard together on developing an important PowerPoint presentation for their agency. Alice was not comfortable speaking before groups. Robert suggested that he do all the presentations, however he wanted only his name to appear on the PowerPoint title page. Does Robert's proposal show all-or-nothing thinking? If so, what could Robert have done that would show flexible thinking?

Write your responses here:

_____

_____

_____

_____

Margaret was trying to learn a new software program and was having trouble with the billing function. The office assistant had mastered the new program and offered to help to anyone who needed it. Margaret thought that if she asked for help she would be viewed as incompetent. Does Margaret show all-or-nothing thinking? If so, how could Margaret respond with flexible thinking?

Write your responses here:

_____

_____

_____

_____

Jack, the new Agency Director, believes his management staff should have no contact with the former Director. His views this as disloyal and has made his displeasure known. Is this all-or-nothing thinking? If so, what would be flexible thinking for Jack?

Write your responses here:

_____

_____

_____

_____

MAKING PROPOSALS

In Session 2 we talked about how flexible thinking can help you choose how you feel. You're not stuck with just one feeling about any situation – you can actually decide how you are going to feel to a great extent by what you tell yourself.

Another aspect of flexible thinking is deciding how to resolve a conflict with someone at work. As we said in Session 2, there is more than one solution to most problems. You can consider alternatives by making a list, making a proposal, or asking for a proposal from the other person in the conflict. Realizing and practicing this helps avoid just reacting to what someone else says or does.

3 STEPS OF MAKING PROPOSALS

One of the simplest ways to deal with another person in a conflict at work or making decisions is to respectfully ask him or her to make a proposal – or offering your own proposal. Here's a way to handle making proposals in three steps:

Step 1: **Make a proposal**

Step 2: **Ask and answer questions about the proposal**

Step 3: **Respond with: "Yes." "No." Or: "I'll think about it."**

Here's how you can handle each step:

STEP 1: MAKE A PROPOSAL

Ideally, proposals will include:

Who does

What,

When and

Where.

For example: "I propose that we each take a turn at cleaning up the snack area and the refrigerator – that we have a weekly schedule, with each of us taking a day."

This is much better than saying: "You never cleaned up the snack area! You don't even realize how much I clean up after you! I want some respect here for all that I've done!"

And then the other staff members get angry back: "You always want to be in charge of everything – even the snack area." And on and on.

Can you see how it would have been so much simpler for the person to just ask for what he or she wanted in the future by making a proposal? It saves all of the blame and defensiveness that people get stuck in, when talking about the past.

Proposals are always about the future. They are not about the past or about the other person's intentions or *Why* they made the proposal. *Why* questions easily turn into a criticism of the other person's proposal.

"*Why* did you say that?" really means "I think that's a stupid idea and I want to force you to admit it." Instead, if you think the other person's proposal is a bad idea, then the best thing to do is to just make another proposal – until you can both agree on something.

STEP 2: ASK AND ANSWER QUESTIONS ABOUT THE PROPOSAL

After one person has made a proposal, the other person may not be sure whether they can agree or not. Therefore, it often helps to ask questions. One of the best questions is to ask "What would your proposal look like in action?" This way, you can get clearer on the Who, What, Where, and When of the proposal. You might even ask: "What's your picture of how this would work? What would you do? What would I do, if you could picture your proposal actually happening?"

But of course, you don't want to ask "Why" questions, because that usually starts up the defensiveness. And if someone's defensiveness is triggered, then it makes it hard for them to think of solutions to problems. Watch out for challenging questions about a proposal, like "How do you expect me to do that?" "What were you thinking when you came up with that idea?" "You know you never did that before." "Don't you realize that our boss will never go along with that?" All of these create the same problems as "Why" questions, because they are about criticisms and defensiveness, not true questions about how to *implement* the proposal.

STEP 3: RESPOND WITH "YES." "NO." OR: "I'LL THINK ABOUT IT."

Once you've heard a proposal and asked any questions about it, all you have to do to respond is to say: "Yes." "No." Or: "I'll think about it." You always have the right to say any one of these. Of course, there are consequences to each choice, but you always have these three choices at least. Here's some examples of each:

YES: "Yes, I agree. Let's do that." And then stop! No need to save face, evaluate the other person's proposal, or give the other person some negative feedback. Just let it go. After all, if you have been personally criticized or attacked, it's not about you.

Personal attacks are not problem-solving. They are about the person making the hostile attack. You are better off to ignore everything else. Of course, if your agreement on this issue is being written up, there may be some more details to discuss – which may lead to more proposals about those details.

NO: "No, I don't want to change the current system. I'll try to make other arrangements to solve this problem. Let's keep the system as is." Just keep it simple. Avoid the urge to defend your decision or criticize the other person's idea. You said "No." You're done. Let it drop. Think about your next proposal.

I'LL THINK ABOUT IT: "I'm not sure about your proposal - I'll need to think about it. I'll get back to you tomorrow about your idea. Right now I have to get back to work. Thanks for making a proposal." Once again, just stop the discussion there. Avoid the temptation to discuss it at length, or question the validity of the other person's point of view. It is what it is.

When you say "I'll think about it," you are respecting the other person. It calms people to know you are taking them seriously enough to think about what they said. This doesn't mean you will agree. It just means you'll think about it. It helps to say a time when you will get back to the other person with your decision, such as: "I'll get back to you tomorrow – or Friday by 5pm."

Make a New Proposal: If there isn't an agreement after the 3 steps above, then the burden shifts to the respondent who said "No." Now that person needs to make a new proposal. Perhaps that person will think of a new approach that neither person thought of before. Encourage him or her to propose anything. (Remind them that there are consequences to each proposal.) And the other person can always respond: "Yes." "No." or "I'll think about it." (There are consequences to each of those responses, too.)

Discuss with your coach the benefits or problems you see in using this approach to making proposals.

Then, analyze the following situation:

EXAMPLE OF A PROPOSAL DISCUSSION

Raphael's Proposal: "I want to change my hours to a later shift. I'm having a hard time getting my daughter to school and getting to work on time."

Supervisor's Questions: "What hours are you proposing? And why do you think that's even an option?"

Raphael's Answer: "Look, you don't have to get snotty about it! I'm proposing I start an hour later and leave an hour later."

Supervisor's Response: "I was thinking about how I could persuade my boss to allow us to do your proposal, but if you talk to me that way, I'm not even going to try."

Are Raphael and his supervisor following the proposal method we just described? _____

Write down at least 2 things that are going wrong in this discussion and discuss them with your coach:

1. _____

_____

2. _____

_____

Would the following be a better discussion for Raphael and his supervisor?

Raphael's Proposal: "I want to change my hours to a later shift. I'm having a hard time getting my daughter to school and getting to work on time."

Supervisor's Questions: "What hours are you proposing?"

Raphael's Answer: "I'm proposing I start an hour later and leave an hour later."

Supervisor's Response: "I'll think about it. I have to see if my boss will allow us to make a change like this. I'll get back to you by Friday morning."

Discuss with your coach why this may be a better approach than the one above.

Write something you learned from this discussion.

_____

_____

_____

YOURSELF

Think of a situation you are currently facing. Write two different proposals which might help in this situation:

1. _____

_____

_____

2. _____

_____

_____

Now think of two questions that you might be asked about either proposal and how you would answer them:

1. _____

_____

_____

2. _____

_____

_____

PRACTICE WITH YOUR COACH

Use your coach to practice a difficult conversation you might face in the coming week, in which a proposal might help you manage the situation. Practice having the conversation with your coach: First, with you playing the other person and your coach responding as you. Then, have your coach play the other person and you respond for yourself – calmly making a proposal to address the situation.

Write what you learned from practicing a proposal discussion with your coach:

_____

_____

_____

HOMEWORK

Think of another situation you are facing with a potentially difficult person. Think of a proposal you could make to handle that situation and write it here.

_____

_____

_____

_____

Then, think of what the other person would say or ask in response to your proposal:

_____

_____

_____

_____

_____

Then, write how you could respond to that with a revised proposal:

_____

_____

_____

_____

_____

OUTCOME

If you actually made a proposal with a difficult person during the week, write down how it went. Then, discuss this the next time you meet with your coach.

_____

_____

_____

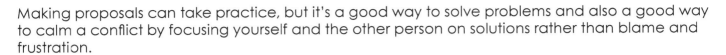

Making proposals can take practice, but it's a good way to solve problems and also a good way to calm a conflict by focusing yourself and the other person on solutions rather than blame and frustration.

REVIEWING HOMEWORK

First, review the homework from the last session with your coach.

Write something you learned from discussing your homework with your coach.

In this session we're going to look at ways that you can manage your own emotions:

Giving yourself an encouraging statement (Your "STAR")

Taking a break

Talking with someone who's not involved

Analyzing your options

MANAGED EMOTIONS

As we face new situations in this rapidly changing world, there are many times that we will feel upset. If you are going through a job change, a move, a divorce or any other change, you know what we are talking about. You might feel confused, worried, angry, or sad. Yet upset feelings are just feelings and can be managed. Emotions are normal and we all have lots of them.

The goal isn't to eliminate feelings. The goal is to understand what we are feeling and to make decisions about which feelings to act on and which feelings to set aside; which feelings to show and which feelings to hide. Feelings are information which may help us, if we *think* before we act. But what do we do with the feelings that are so upsetting?

Before your meet with your coach, if possible, or with your coach:

Think of when your upset feelings got in the way of solving a problem, or created a problem:

Discuss this situation with your coach.

CALMING YOUR UPSET EMOTIONS

ENCOURAGING STATEMENTS

In Session 2 we briefly looked at how managed emotions can help someone through situations where unmanaged emotions would get them into trouble. One thing that helps is to give yourself encouraging statements. We call these your personal "STAR".

YOUR "STAR"

Your personal STAR stands for Statements That Are Reinforcing to you. Write up to three encouraging statements that you can use in a variety of difficult situations to reinforce yourself: Examples: "Easy does it." "This too shall pass." "One day at a time." "It's not about me."

_____

_____

_____

TAKING A BREAK

One of the most successful ways of calming yourself enough to think clearly is to take a break. This can mean excusing yourself from an angry conversation for a few minutes. "Let me just stop and think for a few minutes." "Let's discuss this later." "I just need some time to think."

Before you meet with your coach, if possible, or with your coach:
Write down a situation when you took a break and it helped you calm down:

_____

_____

Write down a situation that might occur in the future, when you might need to take a break:

_____

_____

_____

Write down what you could say or do in the situation above, so that you could take a break:

_____

_____

Discuss these situations with your coach.

Practice saying you need a break with your coach playing someone in your life. Discuss how it felt to say that. Write it here:

_____

_____

_____

_____

Another approach to taking a break is the "24 hour rule" before responding to a situation, such as by email, voicemail and so forth. Wait 24 hours before you send, call or do something else in response.

TALKING TO SOMEONE WHO IS NOT INVOLVED.

Work can be very upsetting at times. When we get upset, it often helps to talk to someone else about it. If possible, it is best to talk to someone who will stay out of the conflict and just lend an ear, so that they don't make things worse for you. Pick someone and call them or visit them and say: "I just need someone to listen for a few minutes. Are you available?"

Think of three people you could call when you are upset. Think of them as your **"Collective Wisdom Team"**:

_____

_____

_____

_____

_____

ANALYZING YOUR OPTIONS

When we're upset, it's easy to just focus on our feelings, which often keep us upset. Sometimes it helps to focus away from our feelings and onto solving a problem. One way of doing this is to write a list of options we have for solving a problem. While we're making our list, we start using a planning part of our brain that is calmer and more able to focus outward.

You can approach this process of analyzing options in three steps with your coach:

Brainstorm several possible options for yourself and write them down.

Check yourself for unrealistic options.

Select an option and analyze it carefully.

KEY QUESTIONS

When you are analyzing options, here are several key questions you can ask yourself:

Is this option realistic and practical to execute?

Will this option effectively resolve the problem or at least manage it successfully?

Does this option require the buy-in of anyone else and can I count on their assistance? Don't take their cooperation for granted. Check it out.

What are the pros and cons of this option? Be specific and ask yourself how important each of these pros and cons are to you. It may be helpful to rate each, with "3 = very important; 2 = somewhat important; or 1 = not important."

What are the most likely "What ifs" and how will I respond?

Is there anything else I must do or find out to ensure the success of this option?

What is the timetable and steps for each piece of the process?

How do my values and personal preferences align with this option?

Write a list here of options for addressing or solving a problem you are facing. This could be your Identified Problem or Issue from Session 1, or another problem. Don't analyze anything at first – just list a bunch of ideas without any criticism of them.

Now, focus on the most realistic options and analyze one of them by asking yourself the *Key Questions* above. Pick questions that seem the most helpful and write your responses next to the letter of the question (so you can look back and see what is was):

Discuss with your coach how you answered those questions and see if you feel any less upset by talking about your options and analyzing them. Write something you learned from your discussion of this with your coach:

REMEMBER TO BREATHE

It's common knowledge that deep breathing helps to calm the nerves and center us. Take a few slow, deep breaths before responding to upsetting situations.

EXAMPLES OF UPSET EMOTIONS

Depending on the time available, discuss one or more of the following scenarios with your coach and then write down your responses.

HOMEWORK

If time is limited, then write your responses to the remaining scenarios as homework, to discuss with your coach at the beginning of Session 6:

1. Martha just found out that Jim is going to be an hour late to pick her up for a conference they are attending together. She is very upset as this will reduce the number of CEU Hours she was counting on for her professional certification. What could she do to calm her upset emotions?

2. Jack, in a phone conversation, threatened to take his chief vendor Hector to court over a minor contract dispute. How can Hector tell Jack he needs a break to calm down and sort things out? What could Hector say to himself before he responds to Jack?

3. Sarah comes into work and learns that her teammate has volunteered their services to coordinate the office holiday party without consulting with her. She is furious as she was planning a family vacation during that time period. What can she do to calm her emotions? What would be an example of flexible thinking to resolve this issue?

_____

_____

_____

_____

_____

4. LeRoy comes to work and discovers that his shift has been changed for the following month by the new supervisor without any consultation. LeRoy is enraged because this shift will make child –care arrangements extremely hard. What can LeRoy do to calm his emotions? How should he approach the new supervisor?

_____

_____

_____

_____

_____

Discuss with your coach your responses to the problem scenarios at the end of the last session. If you didn't write responses, you can read and discuss them now.

Write something you learned from discussing these examples with your coach:

EMOTIONS ARE CONTAGIOUS

Emotions are contagious. Recent brain research has shown this. If someone is feeling happy, others around him or her will start to feel happier too. If someone is feeling sad, those nearby may also feel sad feelings. Sometimes people pressure us to have the same feeling they are having, especially when they are angry.

EXAMPLE

What do you think about this conversation?

Chuck: "Monty, do you know what Sally just did? She added her name to my report, before she handed it in. I can't believe she did that to me."

Monty: "Oh, I can't stand when people do that. She deserves to rot in hell! What kind of report was it?"

Chuck: "It was supposed to be a team report, but I did most of the work."

The next time Monty saw Sally in the hallway, he looked away and didn't even say "Hi."

Notice how Monty responded angrily without even knowing what kind of report it was. Did he "catch" the same feeling that Chuck had? Discuss it with your coach.

WOULD THIS BE A BETTER WAY TO RESPOND?

Chuck: "Monty, do you know what Sally just did? She added her name to my report, before she handed it in. I can't believe she did that to me."

Monty: "That sounds pretty frustrating. Is there anything for you to do about it now?"

Chuck: "No, I guess I just have to live with her sharing the credit."

Monty: "Oh well."

The next time Monty saw Sally in the hallway, he said "Hi" as he passed her.

Monty didn't seem to simply absorb the same emotions, but he still seemed to have some empathy for Chuck. He didn't seem to let it affect his relationship with Sally.

DON'T BE A NEGATIVE ADVOCATE

People become negative advocates for others when they absorb their emotions and just react the same way without thinking. People have different points of view, but this can get cloudy when someone is emotionally intense. The way to avoid becoming a negative advocate is to think for yourself, such as:

"What's my point of view about this situation?"

"Is this really a problem I need to get involved with?"

"Just because they are upset doesn't mean that I have to be upset or do anything differently."

Did Monty in the first situation above become a negative advocate for Chuck? Was he "negatively advocating" for Chuck by treating Sally the same way that Chuck would have, even though he didn't know much about the situation? A lot of conflicts get going in organizations when people advocate for others because they absorb the emotions and act on them, but are uninformed.

YOURSELF

Write a situation in which someone wanted you to feel the same way he or she felt:

_____

_____

_____

_____

Describe to your coach how it felt to have someone pressure you to have the same feeling that they were having. Explain how you handled the situation. (Did you have the same feeling?) Write down how you would have preferred that the other person handled the situation.

_____

_____

_____

_____

Write a situation in which you pressured someone to feel the same as you felt (we all have):

_____

_____

_____

_____

Discuss with your coach why you wanted another person to feel the same way as you did. Did you want them to take your side, just to feel better? Discuss whether the person agreed with you or was able to have his or her own feelings about the situation. Discuss another way you could have dealt with the situation.

Discuss with your coach how you can become aware sooner of picking up someone else's feelings, moods, or behaviors.

Think of two things you can tell yourself to help you avoid picking up other people's feelings without realizing it or becoming a negative advocate:

How can you protect others from your upset emotions during an angry or frustrating time at work? Describe how you might do this:

CALM OTHER PEOPLE'S UPSET EMOTIONS

We can actually have a "contagious emotions" effect on other people in a positive way. If we can stay calm when others are upset, they will often calm down as well. The following is a good method of staying calming and potentially calming others. This is especially helpful if someone is upset with you – whether they are an employee, a supervisor or a customer!

E.A.R. STATEMENTS

E.A.R. stands for Empathy, Attention, and Respect. It is the opposite of what you may feel like giving someone when he or she is upset – especially if they are attacking YOU! Yet you will be amazed at how effective this is at calming people down when you do it right.

An E.A.R. Statement connects with the person's experience, with their feelings. For example, let's say that someone verbally attacks you for not returning a phone call as quickly as he or she would have liked. "You don't respect me! You don't care how long I have to wait to deal with this problem! You're not doing your job!"

Rather than defending yourself, give the person an E.A.R. Statement, such as: "I can hear how upset you are. Tell me what's going on. I share your concerns about this problem and respect your efforts to solve it." This statement included:

EMPATHY: "I can hear how upset you are."

ATTENTION: "Tell me what's going on."

RESPECT: "I respect your efforts."

THE IMPORTANCE OF EMPATHY

Empathy is different from sympathy. Having empathy for someone means that you can feel the pain and frustration that they are feeling, and probably have felt similar feelings in your own life. These are normal human emotions and they are normally triggered in the people nearby. (Remember, emotions are contagious!) When you show empathy for another person, you are treating them as an equal who you are concerned about and can relate to their distress.

Sympathy is when you see someone else in a bad situation that you are not in. You may feel sorry for them and have sympathy for them, but it is a "one-up and one-down" position. There is more of a separation between those who give sympathy and those who receive it.

You don't have to use the word "empathy" to make a statement that shows empathy. For example:

"I can see how important this is to you."

"I understand this can be frustrating."

"I know this process can be confusing."

"I'm sorry to see that you're in this situation."

"I'd like to help you if I can."

"Let's see if we can solve this together."

"I'll work with you on this."

THE IMPORTANCE OF ATTENTION

There are many ways to let a person know that you will pay attention. For example, you can say:

"I will listen as carefully as I can."

"I will pay attention to your concerns."

"Tell me what's going on."

"Tell me more!"

You can also show attention non-verbally, such as:

Have good "eye contact" (keeping your eyes focused on the person)

Nod your head slowly up and down to show that you are attentive to their concerns

Lean in to pay closer attention

Put your hand near them, such as on the table beside them

(Be careful about touching an upset person – it may be misinterpreted as a threat, a come-on, or a put-down)

THE IMPORTANCE OF RESPECT

Anyone in distress needs respect from others. Even the most difficult and upset person usually has some quality that you can respect. By recognizing that quality, you can calm a person who is desperate to be respected. Here are several statements showing respect:

"I can see that you are a hard worker."

"I respect your commitment to solving this problem."

"I respect your efforts on this."

"I respect your success at accomplishing that other task."

"You have important skills that we need here."

MANAGE YOUR AMYGDALA

We are very sensitive to other's emotions, especially threats, because they trigger the amygdala in our brains. We have one in the middle of our right hemisphere of our brains and one in the middle of our left. Of course, if someone is real upset with us, giving an EAR Statement is the opposite of what we feel like doing. But it will help you a lot if you can calm them down – and this method works much better than telling someone: "Calm down!!" That usually makes them more upset, because your tone of voice triggers their amygdala.

IT'S NOT ABOUT YOU!

If someone is intensely upset with you, remind yourself it's not about you! Don't take it personally. It's about the person's own upset and lack of sufficient skills to manage his or her own emotions. Intense upsets are inappropriate in today's work world, where we need to use our calm logic as much as possible, rather than just reacting to things.

Try making E.A.R. statements and you will find they often end any personal attack and calm the person down. This is especially true for high conflict people (HCPs) who regularly have a hard time calming themselves down.

Empathy, Attention, and Respect can be calming, because they let the person know that you want to connect with him or her, rather than threaten him or her.

Making E.A.R. statements – or non-verbally showing your Empathy, Attention, and Respect – may help you avoid many potentially difficult situations. It can save you time, money and emotional energy for years to come.

Think of an EAR Statement you might use with someone at work who gets upset sometimes. Write it down here. It doesn't have to be long. It can just include some words that show Empathy, or Attention, or Respect, or all three:

_____

_____

_____

_____

_____

With your coach practice a conversation in which you give an EAR Statement to a person who is upset about somebody else – possibly in the coming week.

Then, practice a conversation in which you give an EAR statement to someone who is upset with you.

Write down something you learned from this exercise with your coach:

One area of modern life that frustrates almost everyone is angry email correspondence. One method of responding to hostile emails in a *moderate way* is to write them as BIFF Responses: Brief, Informative, Friendly and Firm (BIFF).

BUT FIRST, DO YOU NEED TO RESPOND?

Much of hostile mail or email does not need a response. Email from irritating co-workers, (ex-) spouses, angry neighbors or even attorneys do not usually have legal significance. The email itself has no power, unless you give it power. Often, it is emotional venting aimed at relieving the writer's anxiety. If you respond with similar emotions and hostility, you will simply escalate things without satisfaction, and just get a new piece of hostile mail back. In most cases, you are better off not responding.

However, some letters and emails develop power when copies are filed in a complaint process – or get sent to other important people in your life. In these cases, it may be important to respond to inaccurate statements with accurate statements of fact. If you need to respond, we recommend a BIFF Response™: Be Brief, Informative, Friendly and Firm.

BRIEF

Keep your response brief. This will reduce the chances of a prolonged and angry back and forth. The more you write, the more material the other person has to criticize. Keeping it brief signals that you don't wish to get into a dialogue. Just make your response and end your letter. Don't take their statements personally and don't respond with a personal attack. Avoid focusing on comments about the person's character, such as saying he or she is rude, insensitive, or stupid. It just escalates the conflict and keeps it going. You don't have to defend yourself to someone you disagree with. If your friends still like you, you don't have to prove anything to those who don't.

INFORMATIVE

The main reason to respond to hostile mail is to correct inaccurate statements which might be seen by others. "Just the facts" is a good idea. Focus on the accurate statements you want to make, not on the inaccurate statements the other person made. For example: "Just to clear things up, I was out of town on February 12th, so I would not have been the person who was making loud noises that day."

Avoid negative comments. Avoid sarcasm. Avoid threats. Avoid personal remarks about the other's intelligence, ethics, or moral behavior. If the other person is angry, you will have no success in reducing the conflict with personal attacks. While most people can ignore personal attacks or might think harder about what you are saying, high conflict people feel they have no choice but to respond in anger – and keep the conflict going. Personal attacks rarely lead to insight or positive change.

FRIENDLY

While you may be tempted to write in anger, you are more likely to achieve your goals by writing in a friendly manner. A friendly response will increase your chances of getting a friendly – or neutral – response in return. If your goal is to end the conflict, then add a friendly greeting and friendly closing. Don't give the other person a reason to get defensive and keep responding. Make it sound as relaxed and non-antagonistic as possible. Brief comments that show your empathy and respect will generally calm the other person down, even if only for a short time.

FIRM

In a non-threatening way, tell the other person your information or concerns about an issue. (For example: "That's all I'm going to say on this issue.") Be careful not to make comments that invite more discussion, such as: "I hope you will agree with me ...." This invites the other person to tell you "I *don't agree.*" Just give your friendly closing and then stop.

However, if you need a decision from the other person, then end with two choices, such as: "Please let me know by Friday at 5pm if I should pick up those documents or you will send them to me." By limiting it to two choices, you are less likely to trigger a new argument. By giving a response date and time, you avoid having to keep contacting the person. If he or she does not respond by then, you can choose whether to ask again or take other action.

Firm doesn't mean harsh. Just sound confident and end the back-and-forth nature of hostile communications. A confident-sounding person is less likely to be challenged with further emails. If you get further emails, you can ignore them, if you have already sufficiently addressed the inaccurate information. If you need to respond again, keep it even briefer and do not emotionally engage. In fact, it often helps to just repeat the key information using the same words.

EXAMPLE: PATTY'S REFRIGERATOR

You're going to have a chance to write a BIFF Response to Patty's situation. Patty's refrigerator has stopped working – one day after her warranty ran out. One month after she bought the refrigerator, she was given the opportunity to buy an extended warranty for 2-3 years for $50, beyond the initial 1 year warranty that came with the refrigerator. She's furious and has written the following email to the company.

> Dear Sirs:
>
> Just over a year ago I purchased one of your refrigerators. But it stopped working 1 year AND 1 DAY later!!! I was told that it came with a one year warranty and that your company would not pay for the repairs, since I did not get the additional repair insurance beyond the first year.
>
> I AM CERTAIN THAT YOU KNEW THAT IT WOULD FAIL! This is irresponsible and insulting to me as a customer. I am telling everyone how irresponsible and unethical your company is.
>
> I demand that you pay for my repairs. I have attached a copy of the bill I paid for $195 to fix the part that failed so quickly. YOU MUST MAKE THIS RIGHT!!!
>
> Sincerely,
> Ms. Patty Jones

First, look at the following response and write down ways in which it is probably not a "BIFF Response."

SAMPLE RESPONSE #1:

> Dear Ms. Jones:
>
> I'm sorry to see that you are in this situation. Unfortunately, it's your own fault that you didn't get the extra insurance to cover your refrigerator repairs. Since it was your error and not ours that you didn't get the insurance coverage, we will not be compensating you for your repairs. I guess you've learned your lesson now. We have great products, so I recommend against spreading rumors that we are not a good company or you could face strong action from us.
> Good Luck!   Mary, Your Customer Service Rep

Write down ways in which the above response is not a "BIFF Response."

_____

_____

_____

_____

_____

_____

_____

_____

_____

_____

Now, write your own response as Mary, the Customer Service representative, which is Brief, Informative, Friendly and Firm (B.I.F.F. Response) to Patty Jones.

_____

_____

_____

_____

_____

_____

_____

_____

_____

_____

_____

_____

_____

_____

_____

_____

_____

Discuss your response with your Coach, who will ask you several questions about your response to help you think about it.

Then, review the following response. Would this be a good BIFF Response?

SAMPLE RESPONSE #2:

Dear Ms. Jones:

Thank you for writing to us about your refrigerator. I was saddened to hear about your problem with it. Unfortunately, the company has a strict policy which prevents us from extending the 1-year warranty, even one day (even though I wish I could). However, I am authorized to give you a credit coupon toward this repair or a future purchase worth $50, if you would like me to do so, for your effort in taking the time to write us. Let me know if you would like that and I will send it to you. I wish you all the best in the coming year.

Take care, Mary, the Customer Service Rep

Do you think this is a BIFF Response? Write why or why not here:

_____

_____

_____

_____

_____

_____

_____

_____

_____

_____

_____

NO ONE RIGHT WAY

There's no one right way to write a BIFF Response. What's important is that it is Brief, Informative, Friendly, and Firm. Two people could write two good BIFF Responses to the same situation that are different, based on 3 key factors:

Who the BIFF writer is.

Who the BIFF reader is.

What the situation is.

So the above **Sample Response #2** might be a good BIFF Response and your response on the previous page might be a good BIFF Response, even if they are different.

YOURSELF

Think of an email that you received recently or use the following example. Practice writing a BIFF Response to that email.

> Dear Mr. Brown,
>
> *I demand to know why you are suddenly making arrangements for the annual dinner! That has been my responsibility for the past three years, and you know it. This is an insult to me and to our company. You have no respect for anyone else's job. How would you like it if I came to your office and organized a party and didn't invite you! So stop talking to the caterer – that you have chosen without consulting with anyone – and let me organize the annual dinner! You are a rude and selfish person, who just wants to get credit and attention for organizing this. Just get out of the way!*
>
> *Annie*

Suppose that Annie was out sick for a couple days and you, as George Brown, thought she wasn't going to want to do it. He thought he was doing her a favor to volunteer to do this. Write your response as Mr. Brown without getting defensive. Remember: Brief, Informative, Friendly and Firm.

Your BIFF Response (as George Brown):

Now, ask yourself several questions about it, then discuss with your coach.

Is it Brief?

Is it Informative?

Is it Friendly?

Is it Firm?

Does it contain any Advice?

Does it contain any Admonishments?

Does it contain any Apologies?

How do you think the other person will respond?

Is there anything you would take out, add or change?

Would you like to hear my thoughts about it?

Now, discuss it with your coach. Write down something you learned:

_____

_____

_____

_____

CONCLUSION

Whether you are at work, at home or elsewhere, a BIFF Response is an easy way to save yourself time and emotional anguish when you respond, while you look good to your co-workers and supervisors. It's a *moderate behavior* in response to an extreme behavior. The more people who handle hostile email in this manner, the less hostile email there will be.

SESSION 8: MODERATE BEHAVIOR: AVOIDING EXTREME BEHAVIORS

We'll start this session reviewing how you can use moderate behavior in dealing with the following situations. Then we'll give you a chance to come up with some situations of your own. Write responses to the following scenarios, to discuss with your coach:

THE SHARED OFFICE

1. Beth learns that she will have to give up her private office that she loves and has had for several years due to a facility downsizing. She has been paired to share an office with another employee, April, who is a nice person but on the opposite end of the political spectrum. This individual has talk radio playing in her office constantly.

Describe an extreme behavior Beth could demonstrate in response to this situation:

Describe a moderate behavior that Beth could demonstrate in response to this situation:

Looking forward, which behavioral response has the best chance of facilitating a descent working relationship and a resolution to the talk radio issue?

Discuss with your coach.

Write something you learned from your discussion with your coach about this scenario:

THE COLD MANAGER

2. Nancy is a manager who must work closely with Diane, the manager of another department. Despite Nancy's efforts at pleasantries, this individual is remote, cold and answers the phone (after hearing who it is) in the most unfriendly manner. She does however, provide important information. Nancy tries to prepare herself prior to calling Diane but admits that this behavior is really getting to her.

What could Nancy do that would be regarded as extreme behavior in response to Diane?

_____

_____

_____

What could Nancy do that would be considered a moderate behavior?

_____

_____

_____

Looking forward, which behavior has the chance of facilitating a descent working relationship?

_____

_____

Discuss with your coach.

Write something you learned from your discussion with your coach about this scenario:

_____

_____

_____

THE RESTAURANT KITCHEN

3. Andy works in a restaurant kitchen. The chef, Carlos, has frequent tirades and has been known to throw objects when enraged. Andy feels this behavior is insulting and uncalled for. Andy has reached his limit with the bullying.

What behavioral response would be extreme for Andy?

_____

_____

_____

What behavioral response would be moderate for Andy?

_____

_____

_____

Which behavior has the better chance of establishing a decent working relationship and limit setting on the bullying behavior?

_____

_____

_____

Discuss with your coach.

Write something you learned from your discussion with your coach about this scenario:

_____

_____

_____

THE ADMINISTRATIVE ASSISTANT

4. Jean works as an administrative assistance to Ted. She describes him as a friendly, high energy person and for the most part enjoys working for him. Ted, however, has the habit of dropping work off to Jean in the last hour of the work day and expecting it to be on his desk by early morning. This issue has stressed Jean out considerably. She is angry at his insensitivity. She has had to miss dinner with her family or leave home earlier than necessary to accommodate him on numerous occasions.

What behavioral response would be extreme for Jean?

_____

_____

_____

What behavioral response would be moderate?

_____

_____

_____

Which behavioral response has the better chance of establishing a decent working relationship and the resolution of this issue?

_____

_____

_____

Discuss with your coach.

Write something you learned from your discussion with your coach about this scenario:

_____

_____

_____

_____

Now, think of a situation related to your Identified Problem or Issue where you may have engaged in extreme behavior. **Write down** what you could do in the future if faced with the same situation using a moderate behavior instead:

_____

_____

_____

_____

_____

_____

_____

_____

_____

_____

_____

Discuss with your coach. Write down something you learn from the discussion:

_____

_____

_____

_____

_____

_____

_____

HOMEWORK: A FULL METHOD EXAMPLE

If time permits, read the following exercise and answer the questions for Debbie, given what you know from the below information and what you imagine her issues are. If there isn't time to answer the questions during this session, write it as homework and bring it to the next Session 9. You can look ahead at Session 9 for explanations of some of the questions involved in this example.

THE MEDICAL RECEPTIONIST

Debbie gets a new job as a medical receptionist. She is very excited to obtain employment so close to her home and with such a reputable medical group.

However, within days Debbie recognizes that the Office Manager, Jill, "has problems." One minute she is friendly enough. The next minute she doesn't respond or cuts off the conversation. The other women in the office confide that two previous receptionists quite because of Jill. According to these women, Jill has been raising her young active grandchildren as her daughter is incarcerated on drug charges. Apparently Jill is also unhappily married.

Debbie feels empathy for Jill upon hearing this information, however, as the weeks pass, Jill's behavior continues to be provocative and demeaning. Debbie seeks counseling to decide what to do.

She meets with a counselor and discussed the "Jill problem." After explaining the situation, they begin to use the *New Ways for Work* method.

Identified Problem. Write a statement here summarizing Debbie's problem:

_____

_____

_____

_____

FLEXIBLE THINKING

Think Check. Write what Debbie might say to herself regarding the situation:

Is my thinking "all-or-nothing"? _____

Am I using emotional reasoning? _____

Am I minimizing the positive or maximizing the negative? _____

Am I using overgeneralizations? _____

Am I personalizing anything? _____

Am I making any assumptions? _____

Analyzing Options. Write what Debbie might see as some options for herself:

_____
_____
_____
_____

Making Proposals. Write two proposals that Debbie could make to her boss:

_____
_____
_____
_____
_____

MANAGED EMOTIONS

Emotion Check. Write what Debbie might say about her own emotions:

Did I raise my voice? _____

_____

Did I yell or scream? _____

_____

Did I threaten anything? _____

_____

Did I say regrettable things? _____

_____

Did I upset the other person? _____

_____

Did my anger get in the way of my message? _____

_____

Calming others with E.A.R. Write ways Debbie might calm her boss:

_____
_____
_____

Create some STARs (Statements That Are Reinforcing) for Debbie:

_____

_____

_____

MODERATE BEHAVIOR

Behavior Check. Write what Debbie might say about her own behavior:

Did I insult anyone? _____

_____

Was I rude or inappropriate? _____

_____

Was my behavior aggressive? _____

_____

Did I go against any work policies? (Late, missed meetings, missed deadlines, absences, etc.)

_____

_____

Did my behavior put myself or others at risk? _____

_____

Could I have substituted a moderate behavior? _____

_____

New behavior goal at work. Write a new goal for Debbie:

_____

_____

_____

_____

Practicing new behaviors. Write what Debbie can practice to get to her goal:

_____

_____

_____

_____

Discuss your answers with your coach at the end of this session or the beginning of Session 9.

Write something that you have learned from doing this exercise:

_____

_____

_____

_____

_____

_____

_____

_____

_____

_____

_____

_____

_____

_____

_____

_____

_____

_____

_____

_____

_____

_____

_____

_____

Now, let's put it all together!

"Checking yourself" means making sure you're aware of using all the skills:

Flexible Thinking

Managed Emotions

Moderate Behaviors

THINK CHECK

First, we're going to focus on how to check your thinking. There are a few ways in which our thinking loses its flexibility. It can help to "check yourself" to see if you are using any of the following – what some people call "cognitive distortions" or negative thoughts that are inappropriate to the situation. Here's a simple guide you can use with your coach*:

#1 ALL OR NOTHING THINKING   YES OR NO

Seeing things in absolutes. Something is wonderful – or terrible.

#2 EMOTIONAL REASONING   YES OR NO

Assuming facts from how you feel "I feel stupid, therefore I am stupid".

#3 MINIMIZING THE POSITIVE/ MAXIMIZING THE NEGATIVE   YES OR NO

Distorting reality will keep you stuck and make you feel like a victim.

#4 OVERGENERALIZATIONS   YES OR NO

Drawing huge unproven conclusions from minor or rare events.

#5 PERSONALIZATION   YES OR NO

Taking personally unrelated events or events beyond your control.

#6 MAKING ASSUMPTIONS   YES OR NO

Assuming outcomes based on little information.

*Drawn from Bill Eddy's book *High Conflict People in Legal Disputes* (32), which refers to David D. Burns' book *The Feeling Good Handbook* (8-10).

EMOTION CHECK

When you are reacting to a situation or issue, be conscious of your emotional responses. It takes practice to monitor and adjust emotions. Use the following guide to check your emotions.

#1 Did I raise my voice?	YES OR NO
#2 Did I yell or scream?	YES OR NO
#3 Did I threaten anything?	YES OR NO
#4 Did I say regrettable things?	YES OR NO
#5 Did I upset the other person?	YES OR NO
#6 Did my anger get in the way of my message?	YES OR NO

If you notice a pattern of one of more of the above occurring, then discuss ways of changing those patterns with your coach.

BEHAVIOR CHECK

Review the following inappropriate behaviors in the workplace. It is very important to moderate your behavior, despite feeling anger or other high-intensity emotions. Use the following guide to check your own behavior.

#1 Did I insult anyone?	YES OR NO
#2 Was I rude or inappropriate?	YES OR NO
#3 Was my behavior aggressive?	YES OR NO
#4 Did I engage in behavior that is against work policy? (Late for work, missed meetings, missed deadlines, etc.)	YES OR NO
#5 Did my behavior put myself or others at risk?	YES OR NO
#6 Could I have substituted a moderate behavior?	YES OR NO

CHECKING YOURSELF FOR ALL THE SKILLS

Now, read the following stories and determine if the problem is *all-or-nothing thinking, unmanaged emotions,* or *extreme behavior.* Then, describe what a more positive response could be.

Steve is putting in long days to finish an important work project. His assistant brings him the wrong set of documents and he flies into a rage, screaming at the assistant, swearing at the company and throwing the documents across the room.

Steve appears to be having a problem with _____

_____

What's a "STAR" statement Steve could use to calm himself? _____

_____

What could Steve do to handle the problem more effectively? _____

What could Steve do to avoid the problem in the future?

How should Steve respond to the assistant he just screamed at?

If the assistant thinks Steve is a bully, would she be correct?

What would be appropriate for the assistant to say to Steve in regards to his behavior, after the situation calmed down?

If Steve regularly "checks himself" by asking himself if he's using the three skills above, do you think that would help him avoid flying into a rage and throwing documents?

When should he check himself to avoid this occurring again?

Joanne has been assigned for the third time to clean out the staff refrigerator. It is disgusting. Items have spilled and food is rotting. Joanne is becoming increasingly upset as she says to herself: "Why am I the company slave? Why do I always get this horrible job?"

Joanne is having a problem with?

_____

_____

_____

What could Joanne do to handle the problem more effectively?

_____

_____

_____

What could Joanne do to minimize the problem in the future?

_____

_____

_____

_____

What "STAR" statement could Joanne use to help her get through the situation?

_____

_____

_____

_____

Think of a proposal that Joanne could make to her supervisor about this:

_____

_____

_____

If Joanne regularly "checks herself" by asking herself if she's using the three skills above, do you think that would help her avoid becoming so upset about the refrigerator?

_____

_____

_____

_____

When should she check herself to avoid getting so upset?

_____

_____

_____

_____

Carol has been assigned a new supervisor and she feels she just: "Can't get it right." The supervisor has become increasingly dissatisfied and Carol goes home every night with her stomach in knots. She is having trouble sleeping and keeps running the day's events over in her mind. She is feeling hopeless and depressed. As soon as she walks into the office, she feels scared and anxious.

Carol is having a problem with _____

_____

_____

What STAR Statement could Carol use to support herself? _____

_____

_____

What could Carol do to handle the problem more effectively? _____

_____

_____

Who could Carol talk to? Why would it be helpful? _____

_____

_____

DEVELOPING YOUR PLAN:

As this may be your last coaching session, discuss with your coach how you can address new situations, especially like the one that brought you to this coaching, so that you know how you can deal with it well in the future:

How and when will I regularly "check myself" for:

Flexible thinking:

_____

_____

Managed emotions:

_____

_____

Moderate behaviors:

_____

_____

_____

_____

REVIEW OF MY GOALS:

As you finish, review your goals from Session 3 and what you have learned:

To use flexible thinking in dealing with difficult situations.

My personal goal:

_____

_____

_____

What I have learned:

_____

_____

_____

TO MANAGE MY UPSET EMOTIONS DURING DIFFICULT SITUATIONS.

My personal goal:

_____

_____

_____

What I have learned:

_____

_____

_____

TO USE MODERATE BEHAVIORS WITH OTHER EMPLOYEES, MANAGERS, AND CLIENTS/CUSTOMERS.

My personal goal:

_____

_____

What I have learned:

_____

_____

TO VALIDATE MY OWN STRENGTHS AND PERSONAL QUALITIES.

My personal goal:

_____

_____

What I have learned:

_____

_____

_____

Congratulations! You have completed 9 sessions of *New Ways for Work!*

You can use the following format to check the use of your skills each week, month or whatever period you check in with your coach to discuss the use of your skills.

An incident in which I used my skills to handle the situation better than in the past:

How did I succeed at using my improved skills?

FLEXIBLE THINKING:

Avoiding all-or-nothing thinking?

Making a proposal?

MANAGED EMOTIONS:

Remembering to breathe?

Giving myself an encouraging statement?

Taking a break?

Talking to someone uninvolved?

Analyzing my options? _____

_____

_____

Giving EAR Statements? _____

_____

_____

MODERATING MY BEHAVIOR:

Using BIFF Responses? _____

_____

_____

Avoiding extreme behaviors? _____

_____

_____

CHECKING MYSELF:

Regularly checking my use of my new skills? _____

_____

_____

Something I want to work on: _____

_____

_____

CONTINUING TO CHECK MYSELF

You can use the following format to check the use of your skills each week, month or whatever period you check in with your coach to discuss the use of your skills.

An incident in which I used my skills to handle the situation better than in the past:

_____

_____

_____

How did I succeed at using my improved skills? _____

_____

_____

FLEXIBLE THINKING:

Avoiding all-or-nothing thinking? _____

_____

Making a proposal? _____

_____

_____

MANAGED EMOTIONS:

Remembering to breathe? _____

_____

_____

Giving myself an encouraging statement? _____

_____

_____

Taking a break? _____

_____

_____

Talking to someone uninvolved? _____

_____

_____

Analyzing my options? _____

_____

_____

Giving EAR Statements? _____

_____

_____

MODERATING MY BEHAVIOR:

Using BIFF Responses? _____

_____

_____

_____

Avoiding extreme behaviors? _____

_____

_____

_____

CHECKING MYSELF:

Regularly checking my use of my new skills? _____

_____

_____

Something I want to work on: _____

_____

_____

CONTINUING TO CHECK MYSELF

You can use the following format to check the use of your skills each week, month or whatever period you check in with your coach to discuss the use of your skills.

An incident in which I used my skills to handle the situation better than in the past:

_____

_____

_____

_____

How did I succeed at using improved skills? _____

_____

_____

FLEXIBLE THINKING:

Avoiding all-or-nothing thinking? _____

_____

_____

Making a proposal? _____

_____

_____

MANAGED EMOTIONS:

Remembering to breathe? _____

_____

Giving myself an encouraging statement? _____

_____

Taking a break? _____

_____

Talking to someone uninvolved? _____

_____

Analyzing my options? _____

_____

Giving EAR Statements? _____

_____

MODERATING MY BEHAVIOR:

Using BIFF Responses? _____

_____

Avoiding extreme behaviors? _____

_____

CHECKING MYSELF:

Regularly checking my use of my new skills? _____

_____

_____

Something I want to work on: _____

_____

WORKSHEETS

The following two worksheets can be used on a regular basis, if you wish, for checking yourself as you face and deal with problems and issues at work.

FULL METHOD FORMAT – EXERCISE WORKSHEET

For facing a problem situation:.

This worksheet is designed to help you look at how to deal with an existing or upcoming situation at work. It focuses on what you have done in the situation so far (checking your thinking, emotions and behavior), and then what you can do going forward (looking at your options, making proposals to managers and goals for your own behavior).

CHECK YOURSELF – CHECKLIST

For looking back on a problem situation:

This is a handy short checklist for use in the middle of a problem or looking back on a problem.

FULL METHOD FORMAT – EXERCISE WORKSHEET

Identified Problem:

Write a statement here summarizing the problem:

_____

_____

_____

_____

_____

_____

_____

FLEXIBLE THINKING

Think Check:

Is my thinking "all-or-nothing"? _____

_____

_____

Am I using emotional reasoning? _____

© 2015 by Bill Eddy and L. Georgi DiStefano – All Rights Reserved

Am I minimizing the positive or maximizing the negative?

Am I using overgeneralizations?

Am I personalizing anything?

Analyzing Options:

Making Proposals:

MANAGED EMOTIONS

Emotion Check:

Did I remember to breathe?

Did I raise my voice?

Did I yell or scream?

_____

_____

_____

Did I threaten anything?

_____

_____

_____

Did I say regrettable things?

_____

_____

_____

Did I upset the other person?

_____

_____

_____

_____

Did my anger get in the way of my message?

_____

_____

_____

_____

Calming others with EAR (Empathy, Attention and/or Respect)

_____

_____

_____

_____

_____

Create some STARs (Statements That Are Reinforcing)

_____

_____

_____

MODERATE BEHAVIOR

Behavior Check:

Did I insult anyone?

_____

_____

Was I rude or inappropriate?

_____

_____

Was my behavior aggressive?

_____

Did I go against any work policies? (Late, missed meetings, missed deadlines, absences, etc.)

_____

_____

Did my behavior put myself or others at risk?

_____

_____

Could I have substituted a moderate behavior?

_____

_____

New behavior goal at work:

_____

_____

Practicing new behaviors to get to the goal:

_____

_____

CHECK YOURSELF – CHECKLIST

Situation:

_____

_____

Think Check:

Is my thinking "all-or-nothing"?

_____

_____

Am I using emotional reasoning?

_____

Am I minimizing the positive or maximizing the negative?

_____

_____

Am I using overgeneralizations?

_____

_____

Am I personalizing anything?

_____

_____

Am I making any assumptions?

_____

_____

Emotion Check:

Did I remember to breathe?

_____

_____

_____

Did I raise my voice or scream?

Did I threaten anything?

Did I say regrettable things?

Did I upset the other person?

Did my anger get in the way of my message?

Behavior Check:

Did I insult anyone?

Was I rude or inappropriate?

Was my behavior aggressive?

Did I go against any work policies?   (Late, missed meetings, missed deadlines, absences, etc.)

Did my behavior put myself or others at risk?

Could I have substituted a moderate behavior?

© 2015 by Bill Eddy and L. Georgi DiStefano – All Rights Reserved

Notes:

Notes:

Notes:

Printed in the USA
CPSIA information can be obtained
at www.ICGtesting.com
JSHW060939080923
48003JS00001B/1